Contents
Introduction (1)
The Basics (2)
Test A (3)
    (i) Melodic repetition (3)
    (ii) Cadences (7)
    (iii) Cadence chords (12)
Test B – Sight singing (17)
Test C – Modulations (19)
Test D – Aural Comprehension (24)
Conclusions (30)

Introduction

Having recently spent a year working in the music department of a large independent school with c. 30 visiting music teachers, I've lost count of the number of times I've heard worries about aural tests, both from students and teachers.

Fitting aural in as part of a weekly music lesson is difficult - it often feels like you can barely find the time to work on the pieces, scales and sight-reading as it is! It can be easy to put aural skills on the back-burner and leave it to the last minute, especially if you (as a teacher) feel less confident teaching aural and venturing away from your instrument. However, as exams approach each term, the aural test does need a certain amount of attention in order not to drop marks and affect the overall exam result, especially at higher grades.

I began teaching aural as individual music teachers in the department reached out to me, and I spent at least half an hour each week working on the aural tests with each student. All of them benefited from extra time dedicated to learning and practising aural skills for their exams, even if they were initially lacking in confidence. Practice and subsequent confidence in the aural tests almost always secured the Distinction or Merit that they were aiming for.

While I believe that aural skills are most effectively learned in the long term within the context of playing (or singing) a wide range of music, there are skills on the Grade 8 aural test in particular which are undoubtedly more advanced than can be picked up subliminally through musical practice. This short guide is designed, ideally, to build upon previous musical knowledge and to explain methods of teaching and tips for practising the specific skills which are tested at Grade 8.

These guides initially began as sheets which I gave to my students, with everything they needed to know in one place. Now tried and tested by students and teachers alike, they are delivered to you. If you are one of the students who finds scoring highly on aural tests elusive, I hope that this guide can provide some specific ways in which you can practise by yourself and improve.

Eleanor graduated from the University of Oxford with a First Class BA Hons (Music). She completed ABRSM Grade 8 in four different instruments while at school. During 2017-18 she worked at a major independent school for girls, teaching aural and tutoring for academic Music, and has since tutored music privately alongside singing professionally.

The Basics

If you have got to the stage of doing Grade 8, it's unlikely that you'll be entirely unfamiliar with the process of ABRSM aural exams, but admittedly not impossible. So here is the official information from the ABRSM website:

> *Aural tests are administered by the examiner from the piano. All candidates for all instruments take the **same** group of tests. These are carefully graded from basic recognition of rhythm and memory of short phrases to tests demanding well-developed aural perception and discrimination. The pass mark is 12; the maximum mark is 18.*
>
> *For any test that requires a sung response, **pitch rather than vocal quality is being assessed**. The examiner will be happy to adapt to the vocal range of the candidate, whose responses may be sung to any vowel (or consonant followed by a vowel), hummed or whistled (and at a different octave, if appropriate).*

ABRSM state that *in each element of the exam, ABRSM operates the principle of marking from the required pass mark positively or negatively, rather than awarding marks by deduction from the maximum or addition from zero.*

To gain a Distinction (17 or 18) the test must be 'accurate throughout' and the responses must be 'musically perceptive' and 'confident'.

For a Merit (15 or 16) the 'strengths significantly outweigh weaknesses' and the responses must be 'musically aware' and 'secure'.

For a Pass (12, 13, 14) the 'strengths just outweigh weaknesses' and the response is 'cautious'.

For marks lower than this, the 'weaknesses outweigh strengths', the responses will be 'uncertain' or 'vague', there will be a large degree of 'inaccuracy', or alternatively 'no work offered' at all.

Now that the basic framework is out of the way, let's get into the specifics of Grade 8.

Test A

Test A is complex as, while it involves one short phrase of music, it tests two different skills - the memorisation and replication of a melody (at Grade 8 - a bass-line), and the ability to identify cadences and their respective chords.

(i) Melodic repetition

> *To sing or play from memory the* lowest *part of a three-part phrase played twice by the examiner. The lowest part will be in the range of an octave, in a major or minor key with up to three sharps or flats. First the examiner will play the key-chord and the starting note and then count in two bars. (If the candidate chooses to play, the examiner will also name the key-chord and the starting note, as appropriate for the instrument.) If necessary, the examiner will play the phrase again and allow for a second attempt (although this may affect the assessment).*

As described above, you have the option to sing or play back the part in this test. While singing is easier for many candidates (not having to think quite as much about the notes and just singing back what they hear), some students who lack confidence in singing may find it easier to play. Try both options out if you are finding the singing challenging, especially if there are issues with matching the pitch of the piano which go beyond memorisation or listening for the lowest part.

Singing

In this test you need to memorise and sing back the lowest (in terms of pitch) part of a three-part phrase, which will tend to be about four bars long. The biggest challenge here is picking out the lowest part from the texture, but memorisation can also be tricky in a pressured situation.

> The examiner will play the key-chord and your starting note, and then count in two bars of the pulse. They will then play the phrase twice. You then need to sing back the lowest part.

The lowest part will always be centred around the octave below Middle C on the piano. If you have a higher voice, make sure to listen for the notes and then 'translate' the phrase as you listen or before you sing your response.

If hearing the lowest part is the bit you struggle with, try practising with somebody playing the lowest part more loudly than the upper parts, or have somebody play the upper parts an octave or two higher so that they are more 'out of the way'. Ultimately, we're used to listening to the top part of the texture in lots of music nowadays, but try singing along to bass lines in music you encounter (songs on the radio, etc.) in daily life.

You might like to start practising this test by extracting the lowest part and just testing your memorisation skills. Gradually introduce the other parts, perhaps playing the phrase once without upper parts and once with them included. Eventually, build up to hearing the phrase twice with the upper parts. You can also try splitting the phrase into sections to test memorisation on shorter passages, and building up until you get to the full phrase length.

In the exam, the phrase is played through twice - on the second play-through of the phrase you might like to hum along as the examiner plays the phrase to check your memory, or you might like to spend another go trying to memorise it. It is best to memorise the first bar or two really well so that you can start confidently and the rest will be easier to make up following a correct beginning!

When the examiner gives you your starting note it is helpful to sing it back (even if quietly to yourself) – this gives you the feeling of the pitch in your voice and helps to 'translate' the bass clef notes to treble clef if you have a higher voice.

Last but not least: if you are finding this test totally impossible, make it up. The lowest part will almost always begin and end on the same note – most often the tonic, the note that the examiner gives you as your starting note. If you can make it back to this note by the end, even if you've forgotten how the phrase went, it will usually be close to being right and will demonstrate that you can hear the key. This little bit of the aural test will be worth only a couple of marks at the very most, so do not panic in the exam if you don't hear the lowest part or can't remember it, and focus on the remaining components of the test.

Playing

As a teacher (and in my days as a student of these exams!) I always default to the singing response to this test, since my expertise is in singing. However, I have explored the playing option with a few students who struggled to match the pitch of the piano (and sometimes even my voice) even in simple exercises. While I believe pitch matching can be taught to almost anybody over time, I was usually on a relatively tight schedule with aural students leading up to exams and was glad to see that there was an option to help as part of Test A.

Playing back the response does not necessarily need to be exclusively for students who are struggling to pitch-match. Many instrumentalists are often more comfortable around their instrument than with their own voice, even if they can sing the pitches accurately.

So the premise is the same. In this test you need to memorise and **play** back the lowest (in terms of pitch) part of a three-part phrase, which will tend to be about four bars long. The biggest challenge here, as when you sing, is picking out the lowest part from the texture, but memorisation can also be tricky in a pressured situation. The tips in the singing section above are largely applicable to help here.

When you play, you also probably need to think a little more about the phrase in terms of its intervals (pitch differences between the notes of the melody). Additionally, it's useful to think before you start about which notes are likely to be in the phrase once you know what key the phrase is in - the examiner will play and name the key chord, at which point it is worth thinking of the accidentals found in this key. This will be especially helpful if you have to do some improvisation in your playing back of the phrase!

I found it helpful to practise with students the playing-back of short phrases without accompaniment in different ranges of the piano, just to get accustomed to the idea of playing by ear and 'translating' the range when applicable for your instrument. Then, the process of listening for the lowest part can become the main focus.

(ii) Cadences

> *To identify the cadence at the end of a continuing phrase as perfect, imperfect, interrupted or plagal. The phrase will be in a major or minor key and will be played twice by the examiner. The chords forming the cadence will be limited to the tonic (root position, first or second inversions), supertonic (root position or first inversion), subdominant (root position), dominant (root position, first or second inversions), dominant seventh (root position) or submediant (root position). Before the first playing, the examiner will play the key-chord.*

The aim of this test is to identify the cadence at the end of a continuing phrase as **perfect, imperfect, interrupted** or **plagal**. Plagal cadences are new at Grade 8, the others are part of the Grade 7 aural test.

The chords comprising the cadences will be limited to:
  Tonic (in *root position, first* or *second inversion*) - Chord I
  Supertonic (in *root position* or *first inversion*) - Chord II
  Subdominant (in *root position*) - Chord IV
  Dominant (in *root position, first* or *second inversion*) - Chord V
  Dominant 7th (in *root position*) - Chord V7
  Submediant (in *root position*) - Chord IV

The examiner plays the key chord to start with, before playing the phrase twice through. The phrase can be in a major or a minor key. You need to identify the cadence. The possibilities are:

Perfect

Chord V (dominant, in any inversion including a dominant 7th) to Chord I, (tonic, in root position).
This cadence is what you might 'expect' and it sounds final, like the answer to a question and as if the music has come to an end.
The last chord is the key chord (the one that the examiner plays before the phrase), so if you keep the tonic note in mind (or even hum it) throughout the phrase then it will fit nicely into the final chord.

Taking examples from the second movement of Mozart's Piano Concerto No. 23, an example of a perfect cadence in a minor key is provided as Fig. 1 below.

Fig. 1

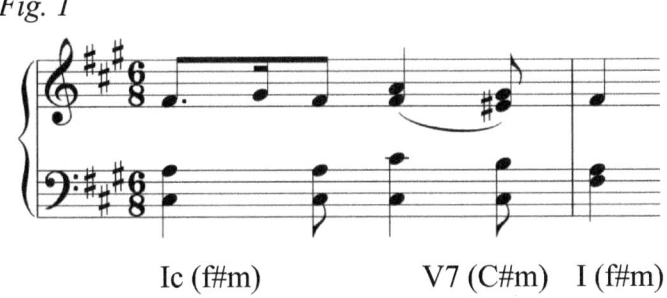

Ic (f#m)　　　　V7 (C#m)　I (f#m)

Imperfect

Any chord (but usually chord I, chord II or chord IV) to Chord V (in root position).
This cadence sounds incomplete, like it needs another phrase to finalise it.
If you try to fit the tonic note into the final chord it won't work, a good sign that it's an imperfect cadence.

An example of an interrupted cadence from the second movement of Mozart's Piano Concerto No. 23 occurs in bars 3-4, Fig. 2 below. The suspensions obscure the harmony a little, but it is a conventional IIb / Ic / V imperfect cadence.

Fig. 2

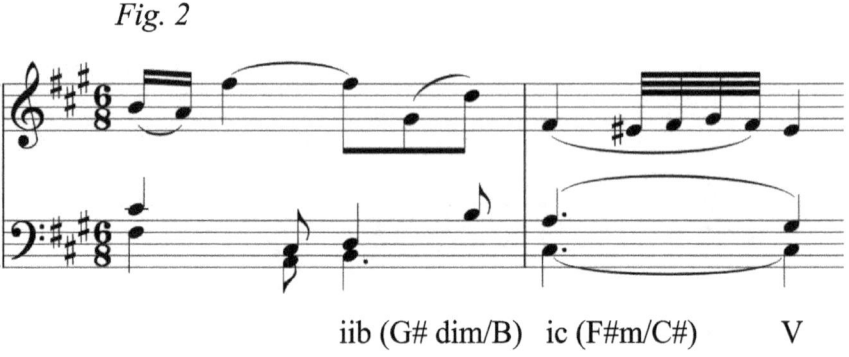

iib (G# dim/B)   ic (F#m/C#)   V

You will find plentiful examples of both perfect and imperfect cadences in most types of Western music!

Interrupted

Chord V (in any inversion, including a dominant 7th) to Chord VI (in root position).
This cadence sounds surprising, like it's about to be a perfect cadence (because it starts with Chord V) but then it's not! It is also known as a 'deceptive' cadence, as the top voice usually fulfils the expectation of going from the supertonic/leading note to the tonic, but the bass voice defies expectation by going from the dominant to the submediant instead of the tonic, as expected. If the phrase is in a major key, this will end with a minor chord, and if the phrase is in a minor key, this will end with a major chord.
If you hum the tonic note it will fit into this chord as the third.

The interrupted cadence in bars 63-64 of the second movement of Mozart's Piano Concerto No. 23 is a popular minor-key example (Fig. 3). The approach to the cadence is identical to perfect cadences heard earlier in the movement, such as in bars 11-12 (Fig. 1, above), but this time Mozart harmonizes the melody with a surprising interrupted cadence. In this instance, this is a chord of D major (chord VI) within the key of F# minor.

Fig. 3

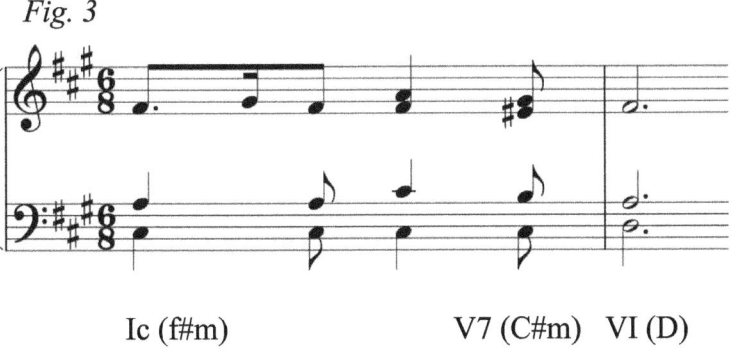

Ic (f#m)   V7 (C#m) VI (D)

Plagal

Chord IV (in any inversion) to Chord I (in root position).
This cadence sounds final but more gentle than a perfect cadence, like the 'Amen' in lots of hymns.
If you hum the tonic note it will fit into this chord as the dominant note.

Most clear examples of plagal cadences occur within church music, such as hymns, oratorios and cantatas. There are many within Handel's *Messiah*, such as at the end of the first choral movement 'And the Glory of the Lord' (Fig. 4). Additionally, the famous 'Hallelujah' chorus contains plagal cadences within most of its phrases in the 'Hallelujah' statements (Fig. 5).

Fig. 4

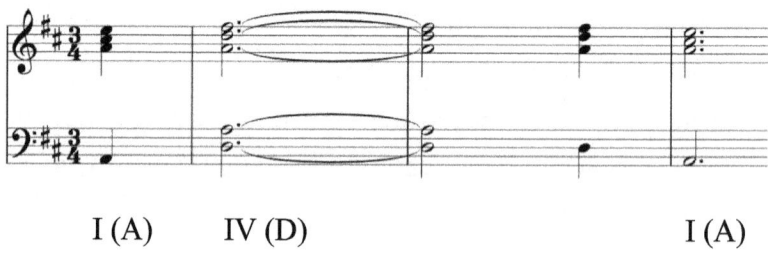

I (A)   IV (D)   I (A)

Fig. 5

HAL - LE - LU - JAH!

I   IV   I
(D)   (G) (D)

(iii) Cadence Chords

To identify the three chords (including their positions) forming the above cadential progression. The chords will be limited to the tonic (root position, first or second inversions), supertonic (root position or first inversion), subdominant (root position), dominant (root position, first or second inversion), dominant seventh (root position) or submediant (root position). First the examiner will name and play the key-chord, then play the three chords in sequence, finally playing each chord individually, pausing for the candidate to identify it. The candidate may answer using technical names (tonic, first inversion, etc.), chord numbers (Ib, etc.) or letter names (C major in first inversion, etc.).

Now that you've identified the cadence, you need to identify the three chords which form it. Refer back to the chords which might be used, and how they fit into each type of cadence. Knowing which chords make up cadences can help you to answer the previous question, and this part will equally be easier if you know which cadence has been played. It is really important to listen to the bass note progressions and chord inversions, as you need to name the three chords which make up the cadence rather than just the two named in the previous section.

The examiner will firstly play the key chord again, then the three chords are played in order, then each chord is played separately. You should name each chord straight after it's played separately.

These are the most common chord progressions for each cadence:
In examples, upper case signifies a major chord, lower case signifies a minor chord. Inversions are shown with letters: 'b' signifies first inversion, 'c' signifies second inversion.

Perfect   Ic, V, I   OR   IV (or) IIb, V, I

Dominant (V) chords in a perfect cadence may include a minor seventh (F in the chord of G major for C major, D in the chord of E major for A minor), making them a dominant seventh chord.

In C major:

Ic   V   I

The bass note here is the same in the first and second chords, before rising by a fourth, or descending by a fifth, to the final chord.

IV   iib   V   I

The bass note here rises by one note from the first to the second chord, before rising by a fourth or descending by a fifth to the final chord. The first chord can be chord IV or IIb and have the same bass progression, as shown.

In A minor:

ic   V   i

The bass note here is the same in the first and second chords, before rising by a fourth, or descending by a fifth, to the final chord.

iv   iib   V   i

The bass note here rises by one note from the first to the second chord, before rising by a fourth or descending by a fifth to the final chord. The first chord can be chord IV or IIb and have the same bass progression, as shown.

Imperfect   Vb, I, V   OR   I, Ic, V   OR   VI, IIb/IV, V

In C major:

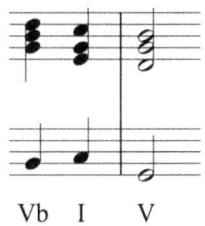

The bass note here rises by one tone between the first and second chords, before falling by a fourth or rising by a fifth.

The bass note here rises a fifth/descends a fourth between the first and second chords, then stays the same between the second and third chords.

The first chord here sounds minor/major (opposite to the key), and the bass line first descends by a third then rises by a tone.
The bass line would be identical and the chord above slightly altered if iib was replaced by IV.

In A minor:

The bass note here rises one tone between the first and second chords, before falling by a fourth or rising by a fifth.

The bass note here rises a fifth/descends a fourth between the first and second chords, then stays the same between the second and third chords.

VI iv iib V

The first chord here sounds minor/major (opposite to the key), and the bass line first descends by a third then rises by a tone. The bass line would be identical and the chord above slightly altered if chord iib was replaced by IV.

Interrupted   IV or IIb, V, VI   **OR**   Ic, V, VI

Dominant (V) chords in an interrupted cadence may include a minor seventh (F in the chord of G major for C major, D in the chord of E major for A minor), making them a dominant seventh chord.

In C major:

IV iib V   vi

The bass note here rises by a tone between each of the chords.

Ic   V   vi

The bass note here is the same between the first two chords then rises by a tone before the last chord.

In A minor:

iv iib V   VI

The bass note here rises by a tone between each of the chords.

The bass note here is the same between the first two chords then rises by a tone before the last chord.

ic   V   VI

Plagal Ib, IV, I   **OR**   Ic, IV, I   **OR**   VI, IV, I

In C major:

The bass note here rises by a tone from the first to the second chord, before descending by a fourth for the last chord.

Ib   IV   I

The bass note here goes down by a tone from the first to the second chord, before descending by a fourth for the last chord.

Ic   IV   I

The first chord here sounds minor, and the bass line falls on each chord movement.

VI   IV   I

In A minor:

The bass note here rises by a tone from the first to the second chord, before descending by a fourth for the last chord.

Ib IV I

The bass note here goes down by a tone from the first to the second chord, before descending by a fourth for the last chord.

Ic IV I

The first chord here sounds major, and the bass line falls on each chord movement.

VI IV I

Test B

To sing the lower *part of a two-part phrase from score, with the upper part played by the examiner. The candidate may choose to sing from treble or bass clef. The lower part will be within the range of an octave, in a major or minor key with up to four sharps or flats. First the examiner will name and play the key-chord and the starting note and then give the pulse. A brief period of preparation will follow during which the candidate may sing out loud. The examiner will play the key-chord and the starting note again and then count in two bars. If necessary, the examiner will allow a second attempt (although this may affect the assessment).*

This is a sight-singing test. You need to sight-sing the lower part of a two-part phrase from the score while the examiner plays the upper part.

First the examiner will name and play the key-chord and the starting note, then give the pulse. You will have about 15-20 seconds to try it out beforehand and look at the notes. You can sing in this preparation time if you like. The examiner will then play the chord and starting note again and count in two bars. Make sure you've got your starting note right! It might help to sing the starting note before the test begins so that you have a sense of where it sits within your voice.

Make sure to sing loudly enough that you can be heard over the sound of the piano, but do listen to the piano to make sure you're fitting in with the rhythm/intonation. Don't be embarrassed about singing, and make sure to sing the higher notes especially confidently even if you don't think they sound nice – the sound doesn't matter, but confidence in the note that you're singing does.

Interval training:

Certain intervals can be identified by the way that they sound in popular and famous songs – you can find examples in your exam pieces, or music that you like, to help with this but here are some starting examples:

3rd (Ascending) - 'So Long, Farewell' (from *The Sound of Music*)
3rd (Descending) – 'Cuckoo'
4th (Ascending) – '*O Little* town of Bethlehem' (carol)
5th (Ascending) – '*Dear Lord* and Father of Mankind' (hymn)
6th (Ascending) – '*My bonnie* lies over the ocean' (folk song)
7th (Ascending) – '*There's a* place for us' (from 'Somewhere', *West Side Story*)

There isn't much detail in this section, as the best tip I can give is practice! You could practise singing your line along with the piano, without the other part, or singing with another person.

Test C

To identify whether the modulations at the end of two different passages are to the dominant, subdominant or relative minor/major. The first passage will begin in a major key and the second will begin in a minor key; each passage will be played once by the examiner. Before playing each passage, the examiner will name and play the starting key-chord. The candidate may answer using technical names (dominant*, subdominant, relative minor/major) or the letter name of the new key. (* Minor-key passages may modulate to the dominant major or minor but the candidate is only required to specify 'dominant' in such cases.)

Modulations – identify the modulation at the end of two different passages, the first in a major key and the second in a minor key. Each phrase will only be played once.

The music will only modulate to three places: the **subdominant**, the **dominant** or the **relative minor/major.**

Modulations can be thought of in terms of direction - imagine that you are facing straight ahead; this is the tonic. To your left hand side is the subdominant, and to your right hand side is the dominant. If you rotate in either direction and settle in that key with a perfect cadence, you have modulated.

Like when screwing a lid onto something, a turn to the right makes it tighter, and to the left makes it looser. This is sort of how it feels musically. The music feels as if it gets higher and tighter when it modulates to the dominant, and as if it gets lower and looser (more relaxed) when it modulates to the subdominant.

The **circle of fifths** in music means that, if you turn to the right (or to the left) twelve times in a row, you will modulate back to the original key! This isn't strictly something you need to know for Grade 8 aural, but it is useful in terms of imagining the structure of keys and how modulation works.

Modulations can also be spotted through the common notes that the new key shares with the old tonic, and also through the notes which are chromaticised (have an accidental added) to shift towards the new key. These are explained within the individual cases below.

SUBDOMINANT

In a *major key*, the music sounds slightly 'lowered' (adding flats/naturals) and more subdued. In a major key the 7th would usually be sharp/natural (high) but during the modulation it is flattened/lowered. If you keep the tonic note in mind (whether by humming it or just imagining it) it will fit into the new key chord, as the dominant of the new tonic.

In the example below, Fig. 1, C begins as chord I. The second chord is chord I7 in C major, but acts as a pivot chord as it is also chord V7 in F major, the subdominant. This chord may also just be a second iteration of C major without an added seventh, although the seventh is usually added for emphasis in modulation cadences. The B flat (or its equivalent in other major keys) is the note to listen out for, as the piece should begin with B naturals (as expected in C major) before flattening them to modulate to the subdominant.
You can also see that the note of C is common to both the original and new tonic keys.

Fig. 1

C   C7   F

In a *minor key*, the music sounds slightly more like it's going upwards (the tonic minor becomes major and the dominant of the new minor key). The flat (low) third of the tonic key is raised to become sharp/natural (high).

If you keep the tonic note in mind, again, it will fit into the new key chord as the dominant of the new tonic.

In the example below, Fig. 2, A minor begins as chord i. The second chord is chord I in A, but acts as a pivot chord as it is also chord V in F major, the subdominant. The C sharp (or its equivalent in other minor keys) is the note to listen out for, as the piece will begin with C naturals, in A minor, before sharpening them to modulate to the subdominant.
You can also see that the note of A is common to both the original and new tonic keys.

Fig. 2

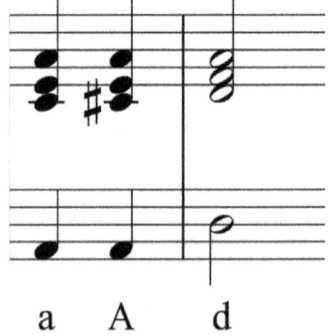

a   A   d

DOMINANT

In a *major key*, the music sounds happy and sharpened (higher, adding sharps), as if it is getting tighter. In a major key the fourth would usually be flat/natural (low) and this is sharpened to turn chord II into the dominant chord for the new key (based on the original chord V). If you hum the tonic note, it will not fit into the new tonic key at the end. This is a very good indicator that you have modulated to the dominant!

In the example below, Fig. 3, you can see that the F natural/F sharp chromaticisation (or equivalent in other major keys) is crucial to the modulation. D minor is chord ii in C major, and when you raise the third to make it D major it becomes chord II. It then acts as a pivot to G major as it becomes chord V of the dominant key.

Fig. 3

C   d   D   G

In a *minor key*, the music also adds a sharp to (raises) the fourth note (as in a major key) to form the dominant of the new key. It also raises the sixth note (submediant), to become the high second (supertonic) note in the new key. (E.g. in A minor the F naturals become F sharps for E minor).

The original tonic note will not fit into the new key if you hum it throughout.

The example below, Fig. 4, demonstrates a basic modulation to the dominant minor. In a minor key, the music can also modulate to the dominant major (E major, in the example below). You can simply say 'dominant' without specifying, but bear in mind that a major key at the end does not necessarily mean that the music has modulated to the relative major.
There are two chromaticisations in a minor dominant modulation - the fourth (in this example, D to D#) and the sixth (in this example, F to F#). This in turn makes what was originally a diminished chord on B in A minor into a B major chord II, which acts as chord V in relation to the new key.

Fig. 4

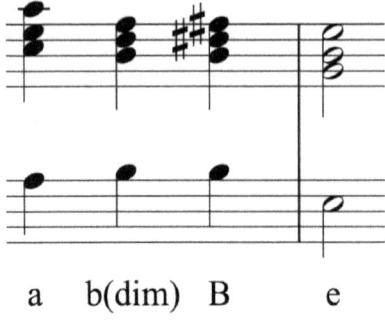

a   b(dim)   B   e

RELATIVE MINOR/MAJOR

This should be the most obvious of the three as the mode changes!
In a ***major key***, it will modulate to a key which is minor (by raising the dominant note, such as G natural to G sharp when modulating from C major to A minor). The tonic note, if you remember it through the phrase, will fit into the new key as the third of the new tonic chord.

This is demonstrated in Fig. 5 below - E minor, chord iii in C major, becomes E major (chord III) which acts as V for the new relative minor key.

Fig. 5

C   e   E   a

In a *minor key*, it will modulate to a key which is major (by doing the opposite and lowering the dominant note – such as G sharp to G natural when modulating from A minor to C major).

The tonic note, if you remember it through the phrase, won't fit into the new key chord.

This is demonstrated in Fig. 6 below - any G sharps in A minor are flattened to become G naturals, which allow G major to become chord V of the new relative major key.

Fig. 6

a   G#dim   G   C

Test D

To describe the characteristic features of a piece played by the examiner. After hearing the piece, the candidate should describe any notable features (such as texture, structure, character, style and period, etc.). The examiner will prompt the candidate with questions only if this becomes necessary.

In this section the examiner plays a piece of music and then asks you to talk about it, without prompting you on specific features.

You can describe features such as texture, structure and form, character and style, period or composer, harmony and tonality, dynamics, articulation, tempo and metre.

An explanation of each of these features, including what you might comment on, is provided below.

TEXTURE

'Texture' refers to the layers of music/sound. Talking about texture involves describing the music in a 'vertical' sense - on the piano this usually means discussing how the hands relate to one another.

Key terms include:
- **Monophonic** - there is one single line (a melody with no accompaniment)
- **Homophonic** - multiple parts move together, often in a *chordal* hymn-like way
- **Melody and accompaniment** - one melodic part, with another part playing an accompanimental role. Here you should describe the accompaniment style - options include accompaniment based on arpeggios, broken chords, Alberti bass, chordal.
- **Polyphonic/Contrapuntal** - there are multiple parts of interest, with 'melody' parts in both hands.

Ask yourself:
>Where is the tune/melody within the texture?
>Is there imitation between the parts/hands?
>Are the two hands playing in unison/octaves?
>Are the hands 'equal' in importance, or is one playing an accompaniment part to a tune in the other hand?
>What does the accompaniment look like?

The texture will potentially change throughout the piece so describe this!
>*'The piece begins with a chordal texture, which develops into a melody and accompaniment texture with broken chords in the accompaniment.'*

STRUCTURE AND FORM

'Structure' refers to the musical plan or order of the piece. Talking about structure involves describing the music in a 'horizontal' sense, looking at the whole piece and seeing how it is divided up into sections of differing sizes.

Key terms include:
- **Ternary form** - the music has three clear sections, A B A, the first section repeated at the end after a contrasting central section
- **Binary form** - there are two clear sections, A and B. A is not repeated at the end.
- **Introduction**
- **Coda**
- **Periodic phrasing** - the phrases are of equal lengths, and the first seems to pose a question which the second answers. This is common in classical music.

Ask yourself:
>Were the phrases equal lengths?
>Were any phrases repeated? Did you hear the opening music again?
>If so, did it end differently?
>Was the accompaniment the same?

CHARACTER/STYLE
When talking about character, it is good to describe the 'feeling' or 'mood' that the piece gives off, and where this mood comes from in the music. There aren't as many 'technical' terms to use here - you can be imaginative!

Examples of characters include:
- March-like (in 2/4, perhaps with staccato and accents)
- Song-like (lyrical, legato, perhaps like a lullaby)
- Dance-like, playful
- Dramatic
- Waltz-like (in 3/4)
- Animated
- Abrupt changes between themes/ideas
- Elegant - ornamentation and phrasing

You can comment about the use of the sustaining pedal, a small range might suggest it was written for harpsichord. The major/minor key might give the piece its character.

PERIOD/COMPOSER

There are lots of musical elements (listed in the other sections) which give you an indication of when a piece might have been composed. You can group these elements together to describe this whilst naming the musical period (as listed below). If you feel confident, take a guess at who might have composed it.

Baroque (1650-1750) – including chords and ornaments, e.g. trills, imitation. Usually written for harpsichord, limited dynamic range, often contrapuntal. Composers include Bach and Handel.

Classical (1750-1820) – broken chords in the left hand ('Alberti bass'), light 'simple' harmony, periodic phrasing. Composers include Mozart and Haydn.

Romantic (1810-1910) – chromatic harmony but still within a key, rubato, (i.e. tempo variation which goes alongside the feeling/mood of the piece), use of sustaining pedal, waltz-like rhythms are common, impressionistic. Composers include Schumann, Tchaikovsky, Brahms.

Modern (20th and 21st Century) – quirky, jazzy, syncopation, abrupt changes, clashing harmonies. Sometimes the piece has a very distinct character and tries to evoke a specific scene or mood. Sustaining pedal, minimalist accompaniments. Composers could range from Bartok and Stravinsky to Shostakovich, Debussy, Joplin, Reich and even more modern composers of the 21st Century.

HARMONY AND TONALITY

'Harmony' refers to the small-scale relationships between notes and chords, whereas 'tonality' refers to the large-scale key plan.

It can be difficult to discuss harmony and tonality without being able to see the musical score, but some things you might hear include:

- Consonance (chords which don't clash) - this usually corresponds to diatonic harmony, which means harmony that fits within the key.
- Dissonance (clashing chords) - this usually corresponds to chromatic harmony, which means harmony that doesn't fit within the key.
- Major or minor tonality
- Atonal - the piece doesn't have a key
- Based on fourths and fifths - rather than thirds as in traditional diatonic harmony

DYNAMICS

'Dynamics' refers to how loud or quiet the music is. It is relatively easy to notice whether the music is loud, or quiet, but you should try to notice if there are examples of crescendo or diminuendo (getting louder or quieter).

'Terraced dynamics' are common in Baroque and Classical music, where there is no gradation between different dynamics, i.e. it begins very loudly and the next phrase is immediately very quiet without a diminuendo between the two.

ARTICULATION

Different types of 'articulation' have an effect on how individual notes are played. The most common of these are listed below:
- Slur (making a phrase legato)
- Staccato (the note is detached from the others)
- Accents (an emphasis, stress or attack on a note)

TEMPO AND METRE

'Tempo' refers to the speed of the music, and 'metre' refers to its time signature. You might want to comment on the general tempo of the music, and on any tempo changes throughout the piece such as a ritenuto (slowing down), or an accelerando (speeding up).

Test D gives you a chance to show off your musical knowledge. Listen widely to pieces of music that go beyond your exam pieces, and use your knowledge of pieces that you've played before to get ideas about who might have composed the piece and when. Think methodically through the categories above. Find lots of things to say and try not to make the examiner prompt you for more detail!

Conclusions

I would recommend, above all, practising all of the tests to improve. This guide would be best used alongside the ABRSM Specimen Aural Tests book, or a similar resource which includes musical examples and perhaps a CD to practise with if you don't have somebody to play the piano for you.

Grade 8 aural is a challenge, giving you a chance to demonstrate musicality in ways beyond your pieces. While you might find some of it tricky, I hope that the guide gives you a chance to refine your skills on at least one of the tests - while you might find singing difficult, you can work hard to practise your cadences and modulations and still score highly on the exam.

CPSIA information can be obtained
at www.ICGtesting.com
Printed in the USA
BVHW040953041019
560256BV00014B/399/P